MUSICA TRANSALPINA

Other poetry books by Michelene Wandor

Lilac Flinder Concrete poetry (Writers' Forum, 1973)
Cutlasses & Earrings (ed.) (Playbooks, 1977)
Upbeat (Journeyman Press, 1981)
Touch Papers with Judith Kazantzis and Michèle Roberts
(Allison & Busby, 1982)
Gardens of Eden: Poems for Eve and Lilith
(Journeyman Press, 1984)
Gardens of Eden: Collected Poems (Random Century, 1990)
Gardens of Eden Revisited
New edition, with new poems (Five Leaves, 1999)

Musica
TRANSALPINA
POETRY SHORT, NARRATIVE
AND MUSICAL

by

Michelene Wandor

2005

Published by Arc Publications
Nanholme Mill, Shaw Wood Road
Todmorden OL14 6DA, UK

Copyright © Michelene Wandor 2005
Design by Tony Ward
Printed by Antony Rowe Ltd
Eastbourne, E. Sussex, UK

ISBN 1 904614 25 6

'Lila, at dawn' was read on Radio 4 by Eleanor Bron.
'Writing Salamone Rossi' was originally written for performance with the music of Salamone Rossi, and a short-
ened version of it, read by John Shrapnel, appears on
the CD *'Salamone Rossi Hebreo Mantovano'* (Siena Ensemble, Classical Recording Company). A version of 'The
Mask of Esther' was set to music by Malcolm Singer, for
two soloists and two choirs, and premiered at St Albans
Cathedral. 'Plain and Fancy', as well as being a poem in
its own right, has also been performed by Siena Ensemble, with 16th-century Italian music. 'Emilia's Poem',
forms a performance piece with Siena Ensemble, using
early 17th-century English music.

Cover photograph Adam Victor

The Publishers acknowledge financial
assistance from ACE Yorkshire

Editor for UK / Ireland: Jo Shapcott

Lila, at dawn

Contents

Lila, at dawn
on the morning of September 17th, 2002

there comes a time
when it's your turn

and the angel arrives and you know
it's your turn

and the angel looks at you
and you sigh
and say, my God, I know so much

yes, says the angel, everything
you know everything

and I have to forget it all, you ask the angel
oh, yes, says the angel, everything
you have to forget everything

but – you start to say
and the angel holds up a wing
and says

remember, you'll have so much more to remember

oh, yes, you say, and then you realise that
you won't even remember how much more
there will be
to remember

so you just nod
and the angel touches you on the forehead with one wing
and you smile
because you have forgotten everything
except that your case is packed
and it's time to go

when you get there
you make little mewing sounds
like a tiny kitten

and you don't even know
what a kitten
is

Mapping Mantua

it doesn't start with maps

they come later
when Leonardo's birds fly like men in the air
to look at the star on the ground

this city, repeatedly like a star
embedded in the day's memory, when the dark has gone

this is the perspective map
engraved on copper, black and white
by Leonardo's men, flying now like witches and birds
hampered by peeling brown leather cloaks
last, loving remnants of the horse who spills
out of the wall
in the Palazzo Te
on the city's edge

the ghetto star
the city within a city
clings to its seven gates

as the island clings to its four bridges
the proud lakes of Garda and Como
humbly reflected in Superiore, Mezzo and Inferiore

it doesn't start with maps
it starts with perspectives
even before they have been invented

Mantua, Lombarda Transpada
ne urbs clarissima et antiquissima venustissimum, in medio
paludium situm obtinet Anno salutis CD D LXXV. ad viuum
delineata.

this is 1575
this is 357 by 492 centimetres
this is an engraving on copper, black and white and colour
this is Mantova, an Archivio di Stato away from that perspective map
drawn by Leonardo's men, flying like birds and witches and
hampered by brown leather cloaks, peeling
loving, lost remnant of the horse who spilled out of the wall

but I canter too fast

blue and green fields stretch away to the northern foothills,
the proud lakes of Garda
and Como
here are seas by another name
Lago Superiore
Lago di Mezzo
Lago Inferiore

bisected through the Piazza Cavalotti by the canal
the mini Venice
with its own handful of bridges

a smaller star within the larger
in 1575 only four bridges, towers along the bridges keeping watch
the Te on its own island, the island Te

riddle: when does a stable become a palace?

two harbours, walls pincered
hungry for the boats teasing the outside waters

by 1628 the colour has changed to grainy black and white
remember, it doesn't start with a map

the century of exploration
of new drawn Ptolemy and Mercator
flat world maps
two-dimensional imaginations of the world's four corners

the stars in the heavens are mapped in the
Sala of the Zodiac, and again I run before them

heavens on earth cannot be mapped, I know, and yet we try

Carta del territorio del ducato di mantova, 1597
can't say clearer than that, Gabriele Bertazzolo

the grainy grey black and white of Urbis Mantuae Descriptiom
1628, Gabriele Bertazzolo from the grave to which he retreated in
1626

beware the twelve winds, trading puffed cheeks, tracing
their route round the world from Spain to Peru
no language but that of the quill and the electric plant dye

meanwhile, in the renovated wing of the Te
the splendours collect with pride

remembering the way their territories protected the water in 1597
the map's discoloured finger reaching along the Mincio up to Lago
di Garda
the big G, Gonzaga

in the anxious damp winter air, the mosquitoes at night bite the
hand that feeds

later maps, 1638, 1704, from Frankfurt and Amsterdam, still show
the slender five bridges, the star, elongated at the Te end, bisected
by water

today you can still eat

the crumbly cake, made with raisins and almonds, mandorle,
bits crumble off the edges, the star map looks as if you could lick
its red cherry roofs, crumble the buildings until nothing but the
flat marshland remains

the city hangs on the water

who was it came here first?
who was it had the idea?

Virgil

first, the unknown man
windblown head across the window, outside
hair, shoulder-length, flicking behind in the wind
he raises, all in a split second
all in a split second he disappears
behind the bricks
all in a split

second, a memory
head and shoulders, in some sort of black metal
exorcised in an arched niche at eye level in
a brick wall, a wall in a square
opening to the right of the road leading to the Palazzo Ducale

the weight of books in his hand
carrying memory is a light thing
more reliable in books, perhaps
at least thought of as gospel there

Mozart waits to be remembered for at least
how many centuries, 1770, when only fourteen
playing in the Bibiena theatre with his father

and two hundred or more years later I am on the stage
while the electrics are being fixed
playing a soprano recorder

light years from the Aeneid, the Bucolics

the truth in the new present
is that a large white (marble) Virgil
perches halfway up the red brick wall

in the school of music a French horn practises
while Virgil nods and thinks poetics in the Piazza Broleto

he sits, a Mona Lisa before her time smile on his face
his hands resting on his book
his head protected from the elements
by a sharp arch
columns to either side of him

in old guidebooks he is grey
in the new Mantova he is shining white, restored
as if he has leapt out to save someone and been
suspended in his own space

Virgil, sitting high Buddha
on the wall

perhaps Jesus walked on the waters of the Mincio
says Virgil

the son of Manto, the prophetess
his father, the river Tiber, the Tuscan river Tiber

his mother gave her name to the city, a city
says Virgil, remember, not all of one race but of three, and in each
            race four peoples

no wonder, then, that temporary harmony has a place here
between visits from the Inquisitor
and the need to pacify Rome
and an occasional Pope

the river Mincius, veiled in blue-green reeds, we hear
their oars thrashing the sea's marble to the foam of a capuccino war

this is only one story, remember

before anyone thought of a map

Mantua, the city which hangs on the water

Musica Transalpina

1.

Musica Transalpina
shoots up in steady rhythmic trees
one trunk carefully placed before the next's foot
a sharp diagonal ahead

you give up
it's all too high
the refuge may beckon
but the trees stay put
pining the slopes
jagged needles protecting the ground

Jakob Stainer
strings his way across the Tyrol
from Augsburg to Strasbourg
and then down to Venice
a nod to Cremona en route

2.

at three thousand metres
the burn
is not yours

large glaciers cool Meph-
istopheles from his greedy task
and slow him up
the mountain has eaten his soul
and even he is considering
retiring to heaven

lattice iron steps
rope nowhere to
nowhere
patches of snow
burn
down the hill
ice and scree
burning down the rock
iron ore burning ice

here the air is thin
as the invisible
end of an icicle
when water has dripped
from its tip

here
the mountains
really do yodel

ice picks
clamp
round the guide rope

the goat on two legs
belongs here
he wears
soft grey hooves
a peaked blue horn
red fur
he perches
on the spit
he looks down
at his clamped
followers

the stone spits
across white

red crash helmets
no protection
on a veranda
planked over nothingness

3.

at three thousand metres
silence is crystal
the air is slow and bright
every sound slides past

you speak in whispers

this is the air for viols
straight strings
facing away
out to the sun
open to the mountain top
opposite
the light flashes the   fifth
the dominant
a major   third
and a minor   third
nestling between
one   interval
and   another
perched in narrowness

a new musical world
star sparks on the snow
as you stroke a trail
between
mode and tone

your leading note
sharpens
as I narrow my major   third
into a modal crevice
through which a wider   sixth
          blossoms

then you hold back
your resolution
you make me wait
you tease me
with   sevenths
and ni
          nths
until we land
in diatonic silence

   4.

in hot haze
the romantic turns seedy
water shouts
too much resistance
at this height

below, in the houses
each lamp cowers
from its luminous aura
stale cooking smells
cling to your clothes
a cough spells the plague

a baroque beauty
turns out to be
the nineteenth century
in carnival clothes
even with the maestro di capella
di Basilico di San Marco
slumming it
down the Grand Canal
by San Zaccaria
in the good company
of Cavalli, Frescobaldi
and the two Gabrielis
father and son

round the back
a maternite Scuola
a children's clinic
keeping alive
Vivaldi's tradition

the Pieta still looks
after its children
for God and the Pope

5.

the sad ghetto
dusty, empty
well in the middle of the
Ghetto Nuovo
celebrations behind closed iron lattices
women behind one grille
Jews behind another

6.

in Vivaldi's church
the church   in which he
never set foot
the organist stands behind the
                                    fine lattice grille
in the gallery

we cannot see his face
                                              only

a crocheted filigree shape
he could be anyone
   he could be a woman
      he could be a Jew

7.

the ladybird crawls
across the tops of the pine trees

people inside clutch the rails
the ladybird's wings curl over the wire
she hangs
straight and easy
bumping elegance
in her wire wheels
over and under
the pylons

at the first refuge
she pauses
at the top of the tree line
then begins again
sheer up the rock face
her colour changes
she merges with the rock
a sheer light speck
chameleon snow

and one day the rock face
becomes bored
with the light, swinging
tease
and the rock face
winks
and bellies out from itself
nudges the ladybird
with its people inside
clutching the rails
with white knuckles

the ladybird steadies
the ladybird continues

the rock face smiles
nods at its fellow peaks
and tips its belly outwards again
nudges the ladybird again

she lurches
a scramble of bodies
she tips on her side
she swings sharp
flat
and over the wire

the rocks laugh
the peaks bow round the valley
avalanches shake with glee
throwing off
walkers sliding
crampons tipping
ropes flying
like stray hairs
falling from a brush

the ladybird finds
her arms loosen
her wings close
she dives
into the trees
her cargo white
bones already

the mountain nestles
safe in its refuge
it hears nothing
it settles
it closes its eyes

it sleeps
in the sun

    8.

a winter mountain
sings blue and orange
and violet and blue
and blue and grey

it perches sideways on a cloud
floating transalpina
looking like
hundreds of colours

the portrait of a mountain is a dangerous thing

    9.

Jakob Stainer
taps his finger on a glacier
for the sound

he strings
two peaks together
and calls them
a violin

Courtly Love

I

so Christopher Columbus was a Jew
doesn't this give you
a whole new view
on an old world

II

in 1492
Isabella, a safe queen
Ferdinand, a safer king
take their names
to be best

until a new shore
releases new names

III

the musician has no name

playing the psaltery
a befitting and delicate sound
for a woman
stringing the others along
while in secret she
puffed out her cheeks
performed clandestine loving
with the sackbut

a secret
closet fipple flute lover
a cornet on the corniche
a cherub with perfect pitch
not an eyelash out of scale

IV

she is not allowed to perform
but she is allowed to teach

remember, I say, that some of us
are perfect
those of us who are three
a trinity
a perfect circle
three steps to perfection

others of us are a broken circle
a smashed stone
we are imperfection
the perfect O
set against the imperfect C
the common time

truth was that in the
sphere
of music, severe and rare,
the incomplete C
curls as confident as its
closed fellow
nothing common about either

V

were you my perfect circle
was I your broken stone

VI

give me time
I said
and note my grace
in loving you

let me divide and ornament you
touch you above and below
circle around
your key note
enter your fifth dimension
and perfect your cadence

let me feel your
greater and lesser thirds
modulate your modes
and minor your majors

VII

I want to
trill your renaissance way
beginning sure and supreme on
your given, written note
and flirt my way
across distance
to the note above

taking you into
history with me
in dissonance

VIII

spot my melody
under the camouflage
of sound

finger my dominant pulse
pare and pare me down
until you have caught my intervals
in three slurs
and a tongue

SECONDA PARTE

I

one day the troubadour arrived
short hair spiked green
round the head, ears curious
to the world, a jagged
prickly pear
from a far off desert
Babylonia or Persia
travelled from
the heat of southern Spain
across the Tuscan wilds

the troubadour has disguised the music
the troubadour has disguised shape
the troubadour has disguised belief
the troubadour observes
that the monk is in love with the monk
that the woman musician is disguised as a man
that the Pope has just had a baby
that the eunuch is in love with the troubadour
for they make music and little else

that fair white hand which pierces my heart
can also heal me, sings
the eunuch
take up thy lute and walk, thinks the troubadour

II

she teaches the feminine ending
the so-called weak ending
since when is the feminine weak
or the weak feminine

picture Joan of Arc
on her pyre, the flames
licking round her rough
unrepentant knees
shouting
how's this for a feminine ending

but ah, says the eunuch
how many of us dare to burn

when dancing is ungodly
replies the troubadour
the earth burns beneath us all

31

Terzia Parte

I

the tenor must hold with the Latin
the three, the trinity
my plainsong, my single melody

I want you to hold me

I fall, I diminish, I die away
and I reverberate
into you

II

I wear a long white dress
I am a floating candle of organdie
a burning red sash at my waist

I stand
my left hand loose at my side
my head slightly bowed
my eyes
closed

in my right hand, my instrument
held to my mouth, my lips just touching
its lips

I sway
I hear the room rustle
and surround the music before I play

and then
I play

III

my fingers flare
hollow sound catches
the air

I flow through
this wand
this reed, this pipe
through which I sway towards
a distant dark star
playing with light

I aim at the centre of the note
I breathe
from my centre

I am an esoteric tune
not to be played lightly
I am proud to wait
to be played

I have circled the centre
of the note
content
to be created
after the event

IV

someone clattered
the spheres
smashed them during
the celestial washing-up

V

feet pad the pavement
bare feet, soft at night
the old skin peels away

I want you to know
there is music
in the Old Book yet

VI

you stalk yourself
you have sat too long
you have danced too little
when forced into the ring
you play the clown
dancing all the wrong steps
but despite yourself
unable to dance out of time

VII

can you hear me when I play for you
do you play for me

VIII

the ship sails
no-one knows if there is
another shore

meanwhile
I play

Shetland

two rainbows daily gave
me a sky which tucked round my feet
tipping me round
as I round the tip
hilled towards the bay
no oilrig to sleek my path
no one-ply sheep to wool me
along

just a silver car winking
shine at the sea
the lobster pots waving
till the sky made me seasick
and the ground tipped again

and me still at John o'Groats

Sonnet

I'm not easy with newness, tired
with another version of eye contact
which reminds me of a day across a table
mozarella teeth and olive tongue

my hot blush is like the boy in a blazer
across the library, teenage sweat
then I carried the Valentine round
for months

now I want to believe that a smile when we
swell within the same beat together
means we might be together

perhaps I've had it wrong all these years
perhaps I don't want to be with you

just be you

Almost History

beyond
the laburnum
presages summer sun
in the winter floodlight
still the rain slips between leaves

still I puzzle at
the devotional window across
from my pool of white night
where an unknown shape prays before
bed

still I neighbour my own past
which nearly detached itself from the future

I now live
a dangerous moment
when nothing took the place of memory

something leached away my presence
when my guard was down
having believed too
many unrecognised lies

leaving me to wonder
where the laburnum goes when
the floodlight goes out

what shape the slipped rain carries
whether prayer works
at least for someone else

Eat, Enjoy

pot roast was the phrase that stayed
the longest, the strangest
time in a land I recognised
from the music of its words, when

I was still into discovery by
default

how the instant
recognition of wit on
wit building across the kebab table

how it bound us so instantly

how it could be not there any more
for so long

how could preciousness be let go
or is it how can I be so stupid
as to want to keep what was precious

wanting to add new dishes to my pot roast
and my kebab and chips

wondering how anyone could lose me
so well

Photograph

the story went that half the picture

                                        went missing
cut   torn   removed from memory's sight
the truth was closer to hidden from history
half the couple not

                       so

                             subtly overlapped

but it could never really work
because her hand was still holding his
the wedding ring edging its shine

the old lady wore her rings to the end
proudly poised near fierce red nails
laid on the sheet
no longer able to stir the dinner
she no longer wanted to eat

there was always plenty
of food in the fridge
fresh orange juice

eventually the daughter in law learned to cook
properly
and even more eventually
the daughter in law
who no longer was
could come and visit with
a bunch of flowers

then the photograph
was allowed   to grow back

Borrowing is forever

You would like to capture intimacy
in a coin
not what's it worth, but close and round
and easy in the hand
that's intimacy

you would like to say
that it's the question that reminds you
to drink enough water
just because someone cares

you would like to keep the caring near you
but you know that intimacy is also
somewhere else with someone else
merely borrowed for now

once a son has gone
he's merely borrowed
and borrowing is as forever
as intimacy

Composer

this keyboard holds its resonance
against all reputation, no tinniness, no lack
of expression

I look like my sister's face in the dark night
window, my eyes in shadow, my mouth naturally
downturned, in sickness and in health
these plum streaks across my brow fool no-one

outside, homeless raindrops hang from plastic pegs
green, yellow, red and blue rainbow the garden
like the cedar spinet waiting for your fingers
you have to hunch to figure where the bass meets the treble,
with
no name for what's in between

I am what's in between
my bass bow, innocent, sustaining when your quill
tires, swelling with assurance as you multiply
to fill the time with sound

I don't know what you think
any more than
you know what I feel, any better than I

I don't know what to call the extension of
our sound, through hands, arms, the curve of the body
to protect and animate the instruments

they have no life of their own
and neither have we

Viola da Gamba

shiny shoulders varnished
slide under my hands as I
stroke each side away to each side of
me

resting between my legs for the first time, some
would find the thought erotic
and I wonder merely at your
seven layers, each hardened
by two months' gap

and now you are mine
I wonder how it is that a man
can lock such sound within you, knowing
that you would wait for my fingers

out into the air, shiny with waves we
cannot see or feel
while the inner ear congratulates the outer
and the hard shine slinks
as the sound slides shrugging
over your dark gleaming shoulders

you wait

Like the dawn I was before

It's called a freedom pass
not a passport to freedom
like the dawn I was before

not a border where you've waited
with your suitcase
opened to stream through
with the other refugees
the other refusees
before dawn, like I was

then it's the pension book
a proud freebie
you imagine it is the child benefit book
again, like the dawns they were
and when you go into the post office
you tuck
your grey hair behind the
newly permanent colour
red, like the dawn I never was
and the woman behind the counter
says, You're very modern
which I know I am or she wouldn't have
said

Writing Salamone Rossi

1.

A city
A city in the shape of a star
A star in the shape of an island
A musician in the shape of a city

2.

Mantua, city of Virgil and Monteverdi
here grapes and olives
kiss
the valley

here the labour of a city
is marvellous strong
walled about with fair brick walls
and eight gates
with an abundance of goodly pastures
orchards and gardens about it

here alchemy makes
a most sweet paradise
a new thing in the land

3.

In Mantua, city of Virgil and Monteverdi
palaces caress the lakes

angels peer from ceilings
apples dropping from their hands

in a round church
an old shaft of sunlight

stabs through a window, high
escapes through a window, opposite

    4.

In Mantua the mist lies low on the lake
cobbles shine at night
a sliver of moon reflects the edge of a voice
an island
a palace
a village within walls
a place in which to get lost
a place in which to find something new

between Mantua and Venice, octaves sparkle in the water

    5.

In Mantua, people are rivers
flowing where the sound takes them

of all the cities in the world,
this is the city in which I make my home

Salamone Rossi
ebreo
a marsh bird who joins the warbling swans
I may have been born here
1570

I may have died here
1628
I may have been something new in the land
ebreo
detta la Moderna

   6.

In Mantua
vespers belong to the evening
the evening belongs to the church

this is the riddle of a life designated
ebreo

thirteen collections of music
the first to print Hebrew music
invoking the curse of the serpent's bite
for anyone who dares to sing without my permission

a new thing in the land

   7.

music travels from left to right
Hebrew from right to left
and back again before nightfall

the gates of the ghetto shut before night falls

8.

something new in the land
a ghetto finds an old foundry
something new, found in the land

here, within a city shaped like a star
seven gates hug a smaller star

this is a city where space climbs upwards
locked in or locked out

steep staircases trap fire
the smell of burning cedar
sounds on summer evenings

9.

these are the variations on my life
my bass line
ebreo
my songs
held between two worlds

10.

Claudio Monteverdi and Salamone Rossi
meet between the acts of a play
somewhere between church and synagogue

it is whispered that a Mantuan wrote the works of Shakespeare
is it whispered that Salamone Rossi wrote the works of Monteverdi

that Shakespeare wrote Mantua
or that Monteverdi wrote Rossi
in whose play do Monteverdi and Rossi meet?

11.

two badges of orange colour, half an arm long
and a finger wide
set in a visible place
one on the coat
two fingers away from the buttons
the other on the hat
two fingers away from its border
visible from a distance
not hidden under a pleat

the badge separates me from the Christians
without it I am separated from the Jews

fashion is a badge
a badge is a gate carried on a coat

12.

where does one language end and another begin
how does a song take charge of its own exile?

I am the intermedio in someone else's music
my name circling between languages
(carnivals, weddings, barmitzvahs, even)
a jobbing musician
an old thing in the land

I am a book lent to another reader
an instrument to another player
a voice to another song

can the reader escape the tyranny of the word
the player the flattery of a note
the voice its song

13.

when a city is invaded, the horses change direction

God dusts the altar and goes home for supper
the harps lose their strings
the walls have no corners

after an invasion singers must have strong voices
to give voice during a time of mourning

the word exile is a large word
sounding like the name
of the country in which you were born

14.

an island
buildings emerge from the surrounding lake
a series of majestic bridges
a city in the shape of a star
a series of gates
a city within a city

someone finds new music along the valley
thirteen foundation stones to uncover
a new thing in the land

while names may disguise the name
music disguises nothing but itself

a city in the shape of a star
a musician in the shape of a city

15.

a common grave in a cemetery in Venice
a rough stone
1631
Hebrei

The Mask of Esther

I

Ishtar	Hadassah
Venus	Astar
Esther	Ad lo yada
Esther	ha malka
Esther	the morning star
Esther	the secret one

I hide my face   where is the mask

She hides her face   where is the mask

She hides –   she

Shushan   In Shushan

Mordecai
Haman
Ahasuerus.

II

The story so far   So far away

In Shushan, the city

lives Ahasuerus, the king   Mordecai, the Jew

Haman

the king wears the robes belonging to
Mordecai the Jew

Mordecai, the Jew,
      turns away

the high priests of the temple

      wear sackcloth and
         ashes

This is the story

    the tale

   of a king

     and the wife he took
     from the people

   and the secret she told

to save her people

   In Shushan

The king wants

The king wants a queen
A simple story

in Shushan
   which of us wears
      the mask

Which of us wears the mask

   in Shushan

In Shushan

III

In Shushan
the sun   the moon and the stars
are made out of marzipan

   Now it came to pass in the days of Ahasuerus in Shushan the palace

53

She wears a crown made of pineapple
almonds as jewels
the fragrance of myrtle about her feet

> in the third year of his reign
> that the king was displeased with his wife, Vashti

She feasts on gingerbread and chocolate
she eats the sun and moon
made out of marzipan

> and sought a new queen
> and from all the maidens in the city

She walks on silver feet
her eyes are crystal
she knows neither people nor family

> He chooses

> He chooses her

IV

Meanwhile	Haman who hates
not so far away	
the man	Ha ish
who hates	who is full of hate
who is	hateful

Haman who hates   Haman who hates the Jews

    Haman has an image of an idol pinned to his clothes so that
    whoever bows down to worship him, worships an idol

Mordecai will not bow down

Mordecai refuses to bow down to Haman

In Shushan
    In Shushan Ahasuerus chooses Esther for his queen
    In Shushan
    Esther's secret story

    v

Meanwhile, not so far away
Haman draws lots to see which is the best time to destroy the Jews

Meanwhile, Esther's people are

    throw the dice   dice with death

Only one person can help them   Only one

    One alone
    One
    One who has a secret name

    Eli, Eli   Eli, eli

    I am the one

She takes matters
into her own hands

He must let my people go

I hide my face   Esther mi yodea
My name is passed down in secret   Esther ad lo yada
    Someone somewhere casts   Someone somewhere
    draws lots
    Purim

  she takes matters
  into her own name

  three days she fasts   Three

  three days she prays   Three

  to a nameless   One

  how many lots are to be cast   Purim

  before the last   One

Haman builds a gallows   to hang Mordecai

Fifty
    Fifty cubitts high

VII

After three days	I rise after three days
Seven gates	I must pass through seven
	gates to reach the king

| Esther's story so far | so far away |

She rises from the earth and the dust

    silk embroidered with gold
    diamonds and pearls
    a golden crown on her head

Am I angry	is she angry
am I calm	is she calm
am I patient	is she patient
am I brave	is she brave
am I trapped	is she trapped
do I choose	does she choose

    who decides
    whose face
    wears the mask

She wears a crown made of pineapple
almonds as jewels
the fragrance of myrtle about her feet

I feast on gingerbread and chocolate
    I eat the sun and moon
    made out of marzipan

    eli, eli, lama azavtani

    why have you abandoned me   eli   eli

VIII

three angels come to my aid
one wreaths my face in grace
one raises my head
one gently turns the head of the king
until he is looking full

one wreaths my face in grace
one raises my head
one gently turns the head
of the king
       until
       he is looking
       full
       at me

The king speaks to her for the first time

The king speaks to   for the first time

IX

No-one knows what passes between
       the king and the queen

Her name is no longer secret
Her people

My people

X

Meanwhile the story so far away

wood and iron and nails
Haman has built a gallows to hang Mordecai
who would not bow down
wood and iron and nails

     the king asks Haman
     how shall I best
     show honour
     to the one
     I most delight
     to honour

fetch fine purple
says Haman
silk that shimmers
golden pomegranates
veils embroidered with pearls
like tears

Thus says the king shall you, Haman

shall you honour Mordecai, the Jew

XI

Mordecai turns from sackcloth to fine linen

Haman is to be hung
on his own gallows

XII

the city of Shushan shines
        with light
        the city of Shushan shines
        with celebrations
a fountain has become a river
a river has becomes a people
a woman has found her name again

XIII

Vayehi biyeme Achashverosh

        These are the days of Purim
        the carnival when the prayer for the dead
        becomes a prayer for good living
        wine becomes dust and dust wine

        when Haman appears
        growl like a bear
        roar like a lion
        bark like a dog
        stones clatter
        feet stamp
        wood hammers
        shell on bone on gourd   which of us wears the mask

        drink until you know the difference between good and evil

                        Ad lo yada

drink until you do not know the difference between Haman
                                            and Mordecai

                    Le olam va ed

cinnamon
grated orange peel
raisins honey and sugar
lemons and nutmeg
a merry tale
of a merry king
and the wife he took from the people
and the secret she told
to save her people

Which of us wears the mask?

in a walled city   in a village
in a town   you may sit and read
do you read at night   do you read in the morning

do you read until you do not know the difference
ad lo yada
somewhere the waters of the sea are made salt
    somewhere the waves taste of wine
    somewhere the sea is chained so that it shall not overflow the land
    ad lo yada
    who wears the mask
    ad lo yada

Plain and Fancy

gold and silver
diamond and ruby
emerald and sapphire

marble, clay and bronze

all arts are learned at the goldsmith's bench

sculpture and architecture

even the art of survival

in my thirty-seventh year
I taste prison for the first time

I am confined in a strongly barred cell behind a hundred locks,
in a dark room, full of tarantulas and vermin
a damp scrap of a mattress
a chink of light for one hour a day

I read my Bible from beginning to end

the diamond is the hardest of all stones

the diamond is said to be akin to water
and just as water may have colour, perfume and taste
even so, the diamond has as many colours as nature herself

diamonds you must never cut alone, but two at a time
no other stone can cut them, on account of their exceeding hardness

rub one diamond against another, until you have the form you wish to produce

diamond must cut diamond

I am confined behind a hundred locks, in a strongly barred cell
in a dark room
with only a damp scrap of a mattress
and a chink of light which creeps in for one hour a day

I see a crack which runs across the wooden door
I secure a splinter with a bite

I take some brick dust which I find on the floor
and crumble it to powder; for ink
upon the brick dust, I pour my own urine
to make a paste

I begin to write a poem in praise of prison
using the margins of my Bible

there are four precious stones in the world
four precious stones, made by the four elements

the ruby is made of fire
the sapphire is made by the air
the emerald is made by the earth
and the diamond is made by water

pearls are nothing; merely fish bones
which suffer with time

the diamond, ruby, emerald and sapphire never grow old
the diamond can never be falsified

once a jeweller from Milan so cleverly counterfeited an emerald, that he
sold it as a genuine stone to the King of England himself

while I was in prison
a man who hated me plotted to put some powdered diamond
into my food

when eaten with food, the diamond becomes embedded in the
stomach's lining, and little by little, as one eats, the diamond
pierces one's insides, and the result is certain death

one day, I caught sight of some fine, sparkling splinters in my food
at first, I gave myself up for dead

then, I took a knife and tipped some of the grains onto the prison
window, near the iron bars

pressing the grains down with the point of a knife, I felt the
prison stone crumble and knew that this was not a diamond,
but a cheap stone which fortunately would do me no harm

later, I learned that the goldsmith who was given the job of
pounding the diamond into dust, had stolen the gem for himself
and replaced it with some innocent powder

*the diamond, unlike other stones, keeps its sharpness even when powdered
the diamond is the hardest of all stones*

one night in prison, a vision appeared
sunlight struck the wall in front of me
and a staircase rose from the prison floor
I looked up, and felt the sun, like a bath of the purest liquid gold

in the middle of the sun sat the Madonna, full of grace and
smiling, with her son in her arms

ever since then, a brilliant splendour has surrounded my head,
visible for two hours in the morning and for two hours at sunset

the light around my head can be seen better when I am in France, in Paris, for there the air is much freer from mists

here in Italy the mists are far more frequent

everyone should write the story of their life

I write to tell the world what kind of person and artist I am

everyone should write the story of their life

I write in the dialect of the Florentine people, the lingua volgare, the language of ordinary people who understand one another

no Latin for me

I am with Dante here

I will write my own story, not the story which others tell of me

everyone should write the story of their life

and so I must begin with the beginning of my life

all arts are learned at the goldsmith's bench
gold and silver
coins, medals and seals
enamelling
setting precious stones
carving, smelting, casting bronze
sculpture

all arts are learned at the goldsmith's bench

from my brain and hands spring the figures of Jupiter and Juno
Apollo, Vulcan, Mars, Ganymede, Narcissus, Minerva, Mercury

Perseus and Medusa

I create the gods with my own hands

all arts are learned at the goldsmith's bench
all arts are learned at the goldsmith's bench

everyone should write the story of their life

this is the story of my life
at half past four on the morning of All Saints' Day, in the year 1500
the century turns on its axis
born with no years
I turn the year 1500 into my very own year
all other years welcome me

Benvenuto Cellini, Benvenuto

at the age of three I play fearlessly with a scorpion
at five I see a salamander in the fire

my father plays the viol
teaches me to sing, play the flute and compose

I am never more miserable than when he tells me I shall out-
shine everyone in the world at music

at fifteen
keeping pace with the century's years
I apprentice myself to a goldsmith
and in a short time, I rival the best craftsmen in the city
in all eight branches of the glorious art of goldsmithing

no bad tree ever bore good fruit, I reassure my father

to melt silver so that it shall not burn
you take the bellows and construct round its mouth a small brick furnace
sufficient to cover a crucible

rub the crucible inside and out with olive oil
put the silver in it and place it on the furnace

you should not have too many coals aglow at first, but let it get gradually
hotter until it is red hot

then start blowing with the bellows

after a while you will see the silver float like water

then strew a handful of tartar over it and take a piece of linen
folded four or five times and well soaked in oil

lay it over the crucible and remove it from the coals

I am the perfect courtier
as defined by the perfect courtier, Baldassare Castiglione

I seek my fortune in the only two ways considered honourable
for a gentleman: by the sword or by the pen

I am the perfect courtier

I am cultured
when I can spare the time from travelling, killing and creating
works of exquisite beauty, I read

I am the perfect courtier

I am a plain man
my work is plain
until inspiration decorates and ornaments
I am a plain man, I fancy

I am the perfect courtier

I wear a floppy black velvet hat, set high on my head
my nose is long and straight
my eyes dark, deep set
a long beard, feathery, over my chest

I father – to my knowledge – at least eight children

I am the perfect courtier

I live the first nineteen and the last twenty-six years
of my life in Florence
I live more than seventeen years in Rome, serving the Pope

I travel to Paris, Siena, Mantua, Padua, Venice, Piacenza, Lyons
and Parma

my country is a mosaic of states
the French and the Spanish think it is their duty to fight over Italy
we are the spoils
who will not be spoiled

the continent is rent by religious and dynastic wars
I never pay rent if I can get a castle for nothing

it is a nice irony that a despotic ruler, such as Cosimo de Medici
can also be a generous patron of the arts

I am, myself, a man after the prince's own heart
Cosimo de Medici and Benvenuto Cellini are as one

if I flatter the prince
and diminish myself
then I shall have the prince's heart

when I have the prince's heart
then I shall have the silver and gold which he pays me

I shall have the silver and gold which the prince pays me
and I shall have the silver and gold which I take from him

can it be called stealing if the prince already has far more than
                                                            he needs

gilding is a beautiful and marvellous craft

*take the purest, cleanest 24 carat gold and beat it out with clean hammers
on an anvil until you get it to the thinness of a sheet of writing paper*

cut up as much as you want into small pieces

*put a new crucible on a fire of glowing embers, and when it is red, put in one
part of gold to eight parts of quicksilver, and with a glowing ember gripped
in a pair of tongs, stir it thoroughly together
your eye and the feel of your hand will tell you whether the gold has
dissolved and united with the quicksilver*

pour a little into a beaker or vase filled with water so that it hisses when
you pour it in

then get the work well polished and brushed with brushes made of brass
wire as thick as a thread, done up in bundles as thick as a finger and tied
with brass or copper wire

take a little urine of children or boys, put it tepid into a vessel and apply it
with hog sables
the virtue of the urine and the sables is that they will remove any dirt or
grease that may have come on the gold

then you may set about your gilding

great masters ought not to practise this by themselves, for the quicksilver
that is used is a deadly poison, and so wears out the men who use it that
they live but a very few years

practice must come before theory in every craft
the rules of theory are always grafted onto practice

to learn how to learn
you need practice, patience and moderation

practice, over and over again
patience, even when it seems impossible
moderation, even in your enthusiasm

after the years you have spent in study
you will learn only one thing with certainty
and that is that you know nothing at all

if a correct beginning has been made, then the middle and end too
will be correct

great is the virtue of determination

I am the perfect courtier

when soldiers invade Rome, the Pope begs me to raise a troop of
fifty men to guard his palace

I am stationed with five pieces of artillery at the highest point of
the castle, with a number of men under my command

we are besieged for a month
I never waste a shot
my drawing, my studies, all are forgotten in the music of the guns

I am struck in the chest by a lump of masonry
the best Greek wine is heated
a handful of wormwood is placed in it
herbs are soaked in it

the mixture is pressed upon my chest
and I am immediately brought back to life

thanks to Benvenuto Cellini, the perfect courtier, the castle is saved

I am Benvenuto Cellini, the imperfect courtier
if anyone insults me, I punch them
once a man came at me with his halberd
I pointed my gun at him
and it just happened to go off all by itself
the ball hit a doorway, ricocheted back and struck him in the
windpipe
he fell down dead
his sons came rushing out
I clapped the spurs to my horse and galloped away

Benvenuto has become Malvenuto

when the poor give to the rich, the devil laughs

they say that one day my anger will be so strong that I will sack
the city of Paris all by myself
I am Malvenuto

I defeated a whole group of men waiting to attack me with iron
shovels, pipes, hammers and cudgels
all I lost was my hat

I avenged my brother's violent death
I have been threatened with execution, imprisoned for assaults
Malvenuto
I quarrel even with the Pope when he accuses me of anything
unjustly

I will murder any man who starts rumours about me

Cosimo de Medici has decided that he needs a hero, a courtier
someone so far above a prince that he encompasses all princeliness
and courtliness
he will be the finest man in the piazza
a powerful homage to God's creative glory
and to the vital energy of the individual

I am commissioned to make a statue of Perseus and Medusa
a man moulded in yellow wax
poised on his right leg
holding the severed head of a woman
her hair snakes whose life has been stilled
her body lying below his

Perseus is a hero of semi-divine origins
Medusa turns everyone who looks her in the eye
into stone
in deference to Medusa, I will not make
my couple in stone
but in bronze

Perseus and Medusa are
Florence and Siena
Florence and Siena
are Perseus and Medusa

I cast Medusa separately
lest she turn Perseus to stone
before he has been cast in bronze

before Perseus is cast in bronze
Medusa spreads a coat of paste over him with a soft paint brush
then she paints him all over with olive oil

then I build a furnace made of bricks piled on top of one another
with many gaps for the fire to escape
I fill the furnace with blocks of copper and bronze so that the
flames can play through them

I order several loads of pine
a slow burning wood

the fire burns for two days and nights

I create the gods with my own hands
and then nature takes her turn

I create the gods, and then
the wind and the rain create their own gods

thunder sounds, like the day of judgement
hail begins to fall

the hailstones grow to the size of lemons
stones so large you cannot close both hands round a single hailstone

a part of the workshop catches fire

there is an explosion and a flash as if a thunderbolt has been
thrown into our midst
I hang boards and carpets and hangings to stave off the wind
and the rain

I stuff armfuls of oak into the fire
I send for my pewter bowls, plates and salvers and one by one
I throw them all into the furnace

the bronze melts beautifully
in an instant the mould is filled
I eat and drink sweetly, two hours before dawn

those who work hard and show genius, prove their worth to the world
princes who enable artists to prosper
are watering the roots of genius

when the rich give to the poor, the devil laughs

I can do any job as easily as sucking a fresh egg

for two days the bronze cast of Perseus is left to cool
slowly I begin to uncover it

the head of Medusa
is beautiful
perfect

the head of Perseus
is perfect
beautiful

everything is perfect – until I reach Perseus' right foot

his heel is perfectly formed
but some bronze is missing from his toes
Medusa is pleased that Perseus may have to limp

I give thanks to God
and to celebrate my achievement, carnival arrives in Florence

in the sky, cupids carry torches, alive with bright flames
Dawn wears a gold and silver cloud
she combs her shining hair with an ivory comb
and summons the trees and flowers to greet the new day

the sun rises in the sky
shepherds and hunters wear blue cloaks and
sing to Apollo, God of the Sun

at midday Silenus, half man and half goat, sings in praise of a
time when there were no wars, when the streams flowed with
milk and the oak trees gave forth honey

at the end of the day, Night wears a black silk veil with blue stars
and moons
in the cool of the evening wine and cakes are served
and then tambourines and torches whirl us all in a dance
carnival has arrived in Florence

during carnival the world
is turned upside down

during carnival
fire freezes and ice inflames with heat
cheats are honest and liars tell the truth

carnival, fat and festive
joins with austerity, thin and grim
they wear saucepans for helmets
and fight with spoons and forks

not for me the Lenten spinach
cooked in salt water
the herrings pickled in salt and vinegar
for me a meal that breaks all the rules
boiled capon
guinea fowl
turtle dove and peacock

spiced ginger
cinnamon and cloves
flavour the windows
where a canopied bed stands on a platform
herbs burn
in globes suspended from the ceiling
whitewashed walls
plain wooden tables
tapestries unpacked from dusty chests
silver from locked cupboards

today the world is seen through mirrors
upside down

nature is the only book from which you can learn art
however, where nature fails
art must be your guide

all works are created with great effort
five, six or even more years are not enough
even for the perfect courtier

I am a plain man

a man who chooses a plain style
a style caressed by ornamentation as the fancy takes him
or is left to its plain devices

I am a plain man

a substance will always reproduce the form most suited to it
I made my Perseus in the image of a hero
and the sixteenth century reproduced me in its image
like Perseus, wings on my heels
for seventy-one years

no bad tree ever bore good fruit
though a good tree may sometimes bear bad fruit

always look for what is beautiful
so that your whole substance becomes an abstraction of what is beautiful
begin and end on the same note

what is left
a salamander shining in the fire
a dagger and a helmet

Perseus and Medusa

a life is a diamond
cutting the years of the sixteenth century
the century of Benvenuto Cellini

everyone should tell the story of their life
plain or fancy

Emilia's poem *or*
The Marriage of True Minds *or*
Have you heard the one about Shakespeare and the
Dark (Jewish?) Lady of the Sonnets?

I

Among the noble cities of the world which Fame celebrates, the City of London, of the Kingdom of the English, is the one seat which pours out its fame most widely. It sends its wealth and trade to the farthest lands. It is happy in the healthiness of its air, in the Christian religion, in the strength of its defences, the honour of its citizens, the modesty of its matrons.

Now there is no discourse, except it be of love

The Thames, the great, fish-bearing river, the most famous river of this island, beginneth a little above a village called Winchcombe in Oxfordshire. It passes by the University of Oxford, and so with a marvellous quiet course to London. Thence it breaketh into the French Ocean by main tides which twice in twenty-four hours' space do ebb and flow more than sixty miles in length, to the great commodity of travellers, by which all kinds of merchandise be easily conveyed to London, the principal storehouse and staple of all commodities within this realm.

London is bright, and shines in pearl and gold

London bridge, the only way to cross the river, is crowded on both sides with large, fair and beautiful buildings, rich merchants' houses, mercers and haberdashers, with privies draining straight down to the river. Or one can always empty a chamber pot out of the window.

Visit by night your lady's chamber window
With some sweet consort

Out of every hundred babies born alive in London, perhaps seventy survive to a first birthday, and fewer than half see their fifth.

II

The City of London is entered via Aldgate and Cripplegate, Lud Gate and Bishopsgate, New Gate, Aldersgate and Moorgate.

In the City of London are Ironmonger's Lane, Hosier Lane, Old Jewry, named so because of old time many Jews inhabited thereabout, and the Stocks Market.

Mercers and haberdashers and goldsmiths, pepperers and grocers, drapers and skinners, wet fishmongers and ironmongers, vintners and brewers and butchers and hosiers

On the north side of Threadneedle Street, among divers fair and large houses, lies the hospital of St Anthony. It is said that this was once granted to the Jews as their synagogue, built by them about the year 1231.

Mulberries, apples and pears, plums and cherries, damask roses and a maze, a bay tree and box hedges

III

In Red Cross Street, on the west side, there are divers alleys turning into a large plot of ground, now called the Jews Gardens. This was the only place appointed to the Jews to bury their dead in England, to which they had to resort to carrying their dead from all over the country, until the year 1177, when it was finally permitted to them to have a special place assigned

80

to them in every quarter where they dwelt. This plot of land in London remained to the Jews till the time of their banishment out of England, and is now turned into fair garden plots and summer houses for pleasure.

Nasturtiums from Peru, Mexican marigolds, lilies and sweet potatoes, tomatoes and mulberries, peaches and apricots, roses and clematis, larkspur, delphinium, yellow foxgloves, lilacs and laburnum. Asparagus and all kinds of radish and a lemon tree

There is an ancient law of England that if any Christian man did marry with a woman that was a Jew, or a Christian woman that married with a Jew, it was a felony, and the party so offending should be burnt alive.

People die from time to time, and worms eat them, but not for love

IV

In 1215, in the civil wars between King John and his barons, the barons entered the City of London. They spoiled the friars' houses and then they broke into the Jews' houses and filled their purses. Then, with the stones of the Jews' broken houses, they repaired the gates and the walls of the city.

A brick can hold a secret for centuries
Bound into clay
Bound over into sworn secrecy
A Roman brick where Samson still drives his foxes into the corn
Which burns in the summer sun
The charred flour mixed with the red brick dust

Black, charred flour makes bitter bread
Bitter, like the plague, the black plague

81

The best cure for the plague is if the queen touches you, for her divine touch cures all

These are the boundaries of reason.

v

Something causes the plague
Something dark and mysterious and unknown

Blame it on the Jews

And so the laws begin

Jews shall worship in their synagogues in a subdued tone, so that Christians will not be able to hear them

All Jews over the age of seven years old, shall wear a badge on the outer garment, in the form of two Tablets joined, of yellow felt, of the length of six fingers and of the breadth of three fingers

No Jew shall be allowed in any town without special licence, except those towns where Jews customarily reside

Any Christian man or woman who marries with a Jew, should be burnt alive.

What are the boundaries of reason?

Beyond the boundaries of reason, the stories begin

The Jews are slandered as forgers and counterfeiters, thieves and castrators and the crucifiers of children

Male Jews, it is said, have a tail, and, like women, a monthly
flow of blood

There are riots and massacres, in Norwich, in Bury St Edmunds,
at Stamford and at Lincoln and at York, in London, Canterbury
and Northampton

The Jews, it is said, are a dark and swarthy people, great forgers
of money, and bringers of the plague

VI

Human life, it is said, depends on the four humours, and a bal-
ance of the four elements
Earth, air, fire and water
Blood and phlegm, choler and bile
Dark, mysterious elements
Mysterious, dark materials

In 1280 all Jews are commanded to go to church, to hear the
Dominican friars preach against them.

In 1290, all remaining estates belonging to the Jews are seized,
and the entire community is banished from the realm before
the feast of All Saints

The saints watch the first country of Christendom whence the
Jews are expelled, without hope of return.

The feast of All Saints is in November

Now, by the ground that we are banished from
we could curse away a winter's night

England is the first country of Christendom whence the Jews
are banished
we are estranged from ourselves

Ora pro nobis

VII

We are banished from our homes

We embrace and kiss and take ten thousand leaves

We find an age of discord and continual strife

A time when words are no longer music to our ears
When objects are not pleasing in our eyes
When touch is not welcome to our hands
To see, to hear, to touch
These are no longer in perfect sympathy

For we are estranged from ourselves
Lacking even a glass
Wherein to see our shadows as we pass

VIII

The Jews do not return to England until 1656

Absence lends a precious seeing to the eye
A lover's eyes will gaze an eagle blind
A lover's ear will hear the lowest sound

The course of true love cannot always sound smooth

In early seventeenth-century London there are over 10,000 aliens
French, Dutch, Spaniards, Portuguese, a small number of black
people – and

Perhaps

Jews

Marranos

New Christians. Converts. New converts.
New Christians. Conversos.

A Marrano is one descended from Jews or infidels, whose
parents were never christened, but for to save their goods, will
say they are Christians.

A Marrano is a Jew counterfeitly turned Christian.

Is a counterfeit profession
Better than unseen hypocrisy

How can you recognise a false Jew
A secret Jew.
A false Jew, a converted Jew, a counterfeit Jew.
A Christian Jew. A False Jew. A Counterfeit Christian.

How can you really tell the difference between a Christian and
a Jew?
How can you tell a false love from a lover's vows

The seventh of September, being Sunday, between three and four of the clock in the afternoon, Queen Anne Boleyn is delivered of a fair young lady.

A quart of Gascoigne wine, another of Spanish, Greek and Corsican wines, ale from barley

Love's tongue is subtle as a sphynx

The child is named Elizabeth, christened in a mantle of purple velvet, with a long train furred with ermine.

Her bounty is as boundless as the sea

Strawberries in red wine with sugar, cinnamon and ginger
Cherries with mustard, cinnamon and ginger
Mace and saffron
Rose water

Eliza is something of a scholar,
and a great out-of-doors woman
when not taken up with her queen business, she likes riding, hunting, staying in country houses, dancing, flirting and ordering the most magnificent dresses ever worn by mortal woman.

She lies in her pavilion, wearing cloth of gold and silver

A corset and a farthingale.
A petticoat which takes three months to sew.
8,500 pearls sewn onto a single dress.

Motifs painted on silk.
The Iris, a symbol of virginity.
Kingfishers, the halcyon days of Eliza's reign.
Sea monsters which master the ocean for England.
Snakes and wisdom.
Strawberries, a symbol of the virgin queen.
The Virgin Queen.
Shall we compare her to a summer's day?

Queen Elizabeth, if she has ever heard of Shakespeare, will
allow him to be a disreputable sort of middle-class professional
person
A stage player is, after all, a nobleman's servant of much less
importance than a cook

There is no question here of a marriage of true minds
Of being compared to a summer's day

It is enough to be
A tudor rose
Eliza
Gloriana
The Fairy Queen
Cynthia
Astraea
Virginia
Bess
Elizabeth Tudor

What's in a name
So much in a name

x

Meanwhile, back in the City of London
The larks make sweet division
Soft stillness and the night
Become the touches of sweet harmony
While families close their doors
Light their candles
And speak in other tongues
Subtle as the sphinx

in the houses, bricks and mortar
seal their secrets behind closed doors
which only open to release questions

How can you tell the Jews from the old Christians?
How can you tell the Jews from the new Christians?

New Christians must be secret Jews, if they do not eat pork
If they use olive oil rather than lard
When they change their bed linen every Friday
When they call their children by Old Testament names
When they pray standing rather than kneeling
When they turn to face a wall, on hearing of a death.

The bricks still hold their secrets

A Marrano must be a consummate performer, for whom
Jewishness and Christianity are costumes to be assumed or shed

The love of God is not a love which alters when it alteration finds

In private the Jews celebrate Passover
in public they attend Lutheran churches, listen to the sermons,
and take the bread and wine in the manner and form as do the
other heretics – I mean, the Protestants.

In public, the children of the Jews are christened and buried in
churches; they marry in churches whose floors are strewn with
rushes and herbs

Perhaps we even play with our own shadows
And become rare Jews
Who have as many changes of face
As are carved on one single cherry stone

You can as soon kindle fire with snow
As quench the fire of love with words

XI

Meanwhile, back in the City of London

Emilia Lanier
Born Bassano
Poet
Whore
School teacher
Wife
Mistress
Adulterous mother
A fair poet
No better than she should be
Alfonso's widow
Jewish?

Protestant?
What's in a name?

A musician flourishes the name Bassano, borrowed from a
neutral, townlike place
a Christian town

The Bassanos string their lives across mountains
From Italy to Engand, when King Henry VIII beckons
The Bassanos find a new home in an old London monastery
Cloaked in new habits, new names, as many as a rose
An old life wrapped like a marriage gift in a single name
Emilia Bassano
A woman who may be wooed
A woman who may be won

Emilia
Born in London
Christened in St Botolph's church
Married to Captain Alfonso Lanier, for colour,
in another St Botolph
Churches whose floors are strewn with rushes and herbs
Emilia Bassano Lanier

This is Emilia
As true as steel
As sun to day
As the earth to its centre

Emilia is a woman and therefore must be loved

XII

Emilia is the daughter of a Bassano

The mistress of Henry Hunsdon, Lord Chamberlain to Queen
Elizabeth
To whom she bears a son, also called Henry

On account of whom she is married for colour to Captain Alfonso
Lanier, one of the fifty-nine musicians who play at Queen
Elizabeth's funeral in 1603
The same Captain Alfonso Lanier who is later licensed to bring
hay and straw for sale into London, to strew upon the floors of
churches

Now we begin to understand what there may be in a name

Emila Lanier is also a poet
The first Englishwoman to publish a substantial volume of
poems in English
Salve Deus Rex Judaeorum
Hail, God, King of the Jews
Salve Deus
The gospel according to Emilia

XIII

Emilia
Perhaps a mistress whose eyes are nothing like the sun
But raven black
Black as hell, dark as night

Even when her fingers play a wiry concord
Which kisses the tender inward of her hand
As her velvet brow
Strings Apollo's lute
To speak of love
Making even the heavens drowsy

When night's cloak hides her downcast eyes
All the world is in love with night
All the world is in love with Emilia

XIV

Emilia Lanier is the first woman in England to publish a long devotional poem
Accompanying, in the same year, 1611, the King James English Bible based on the belief that every Christian should be able to read the Bible in the vernacular, in their own language

Salve Deus Rex Judaeorum
Hail God, King of the Jews

Remember the advice of Paul in the gospels
Women should remain silent in church
No sounds of their sweet music
Creeping in men's ears
Paul advises that women should remain silent in church.

Women and horses, after all, must be well governed
As we do not handle glasses like pots, because they are weaker vessels, but touch them nicely and softly for fear of cracks, so a man must treat his wife with gentleness and softness, not expecting that wisdom, nor that faith, nor that patience, nor that strength, in the weaker vessel.

XV

The gospel according to Emilia

A dark, highly educated woman
A fair poet

Raven black eyes, eyelashes and eyebrows
No yellow locks, crisped like golden wire

A fickle, swarthy mistress, black as hell, dark as night, a dark,
dark lady, who arrives in the dark of night

A dark lady nestling in between the lines of a sonnet
A lady whose eyes are nothing like the sun

What's in a colour

Hair can be coloured black with elderberries or yellow with
marigolds.

What's in a colour

The melancholic is Covetous, envious, black, dark of colour,
swarthy

It is said that the Jews are a dark and swarthy people, great
forgers of money and bringers of the plague

It is said that the best cure is if the queen touches you, for her
touch is divine and cures all

Queen Elizabeth is of fair complexion.
Marigolds are good to dye hair fair

What is the right name for a colour?

XVI

The gospel according to Emilia Lanier, the dark, poet, daughter
of Baptiste Bassano, a Venetian Christianised Jew

*Gentle reader, if thou desire to be resolved, why I give this title, Salve Deus
Rex Judaeorum, know for certain; that it was delivered unto me in sleep
many years before, and was quite out of my memory, until I had written the
passion of Christ, when it immediately came back into my remembrance.*

*I have written these poems, says the gospel according to Emilia, to make
known to the world that all women deserve not to be blamed by those evil
disposed men, who forget that they were born of woman, nourished by
woman, and that, if it were not by the means of women, they would be
quite extinguished out of the world.*

We are women, and may be wooed and won
We are women and may be wooed and lost

*These men have tempted even the patience of God himself, who gave power
to wise and virtuous women, to bring down their pride and arrogance.*

*As was wicked Haman by the divine prayers and prudent proceedings of
beautiful Hester, blasphemous Holofernes by the invincible courage, rare
wisdom and confident carriage of Judith; and the unjust Judges by the
innocency of chaste Susanna.*

XVII

Hail to the Lord, King of the Jews

Here is a woman writing of divinest things
A precious thing which is but seldom seen
Even by a lover's eye

For my courage
From Juno I have drawn state and dignity
From warlike Pallas, wisdom and fortitude
From fair Venus, all of her best to grace
The darkest night with the beauteous face
Of my poetry

On my temples I wear fair Daphne's crown,
The never changing laurel
I follow in wise Minerva's path
With bright Cynthia and Venus at my side
The Muses my companions

For well you know, the world is but a stage
Where all do play their parts and must be gone
By a name, I know not how to tell you who I am

Our mother Eve, who tasted of the tree
Giving to Adam what she held most dear
Was simply good

Adam cannot be excused
Her fault, though great, yet he was most to blame
What weakness offered, strength might have refused
Being Lord of all, the greater was his shame

For he was Lord and King of all the earth
Before poor Eve had either life or breath

If Eve did err, it was for knowledge sake

If Adam would eat it, who had power to stay him?

Not Eve, whose fault was only too much love
Which made her give this present to her dear
That what she tasted, he might likewise prove
Whereby his knowledge might become more clear

Yet men will boast of knowledge, which he took
From Eve's fair hand

Black as a raven in her blackest hue
Eve's lips are like scarlet threads, yet much more sweet
Than is the sweetest honey dropping dew

Her cheeks are beds of spices, flowers sweet
Her lips, like lilies, dropping down pure myrrh

Emilia writes and unites Eve with Mary Magdalene
With the God of the Old Testament
And the Christ of the new

All held within the bricks of the Bible
And the gospel according to Emilia

Emilia, the poet, is buried in a church in Clerkenwell
Its floor strewn with herbs and rushes
A church by any other name would smell as sweet

XVIII

Meanwhile, back in the City of London
pleasure gardens grow

Nasturtiums from Peru, Mexican marigolds, lilies and sweet
potatoes, tomatoes and mulberries,

Out of every hundred babies born alive in the City of London
some may be Jewish

peaches and apricots, roses and clematis, larkspur and
delphinium, yellow foxgloves, lilacs and laburnum

bricks bind their secrets
with reason and faith
shaded by the dark mysteries of the plague

Elms and cherry and birch trees, pinks and violets, beds of
fragrant flowers

In between times of night and day
the false and the real are as shadows in a glass
even a summer's day turns dark when the sun passes

Some of us are estranged from ourselves

XIX

In the City of London
A poem can bridge worlds

Salve Deus Rex Judaeorum
Hail God, King of the

a name by any other season
secret as a sphinx in the night
as a rose without a name

97

Somewhere, in the City of London
A poet called Emilia
May have met a poet called William Shakespeare
May have met a queen called Elizabeth

It is said that Elizabeth led an enigmatic life; she was, it is said, the virgin queen.

She never married, and the answer, it is said, is that, secretly, she was a practising Jewess.

A Jewish princess cannot marry just anyone.

If she is to be exquisitely happy, and Elizabeth could settle for no less, for she is, after all, Queen of England, she must be courted and wed by a Jewish man.

It is said that William Shakespeare was descended from a line of forcibly converted Jews.

It may even be said that William Shakespeare was Queen Elizabeth's secret lover, just as it is said that Emilia Bassano was the secret mistress of William Shakespeare.

It may be said that Queen Elizabeth, Willam Shakespeare and Emilia Bassano Lanier met in the City of London
and feasted on alpine strawberries, nutmeg, mace and cinnamon, gingerbread gilded with gold leaf, oranges and cloves

And jellies of all colours

What's in a colour?

XX

The colours of the past can change
From mulberry to coal
Centuries of bricks
Hold secrets
In churches
Whose floors are strewn
With Jews of all persuasions

Rushes and herbs powder back
Into old stories

In 13th century England, it was said that a friar once fell in love
with a beautiful Jewish girl. He wooed her for a long time, but
she spurned him and his promises. This only inflamed his illicit
love. Eventually, he doffed the garb of his Christian faith and
donned the garments of Judaism. He secretly became a Jew, and
so succeeded in his protestations of love.

Old stories paper questions

How can you tell the difference between a Christian and a Jew?
How do you tell the difference between a Jew and a Christian?
Hath not a Christian eyes?
Hath not a Christian hands, senses, affections, passions?

How do you kindle the fire of love with a name?

What's in a name?

MICHELENE WANDOR is a playwright, poet, short story writer, reviewer, broadcaster, theatre historian and musician. With degrees from Cambridge and Essex universities and from Trinity College / University of London, she has taught in Britain at the Guildhall School of Drama, London, the City Lit, London, London Metropolitan University and at various universities abroad. At the time of publication, she holds a Royal Literary Fund Fellowship at Birkbeck College, London.

Recipient of many awards and nominations, particularly for her radio dramatisations. Michelene Wandor is a prolific, and widely published, writer.

She is also an accomplished musician, performing Renaissance and Baroque music with her early music group, The Siena Ensemble.

Recent publications in
Arc Publications' series
POETRY FROM THE UK / IRELAND
edited by Jo Shapcott
include:

LIZ ALMOND
The Shut Drawer

JONATHAN ASSER
Outside The All Stars

DONALD ATKINSON
In Waterlight: Poems New, Selected & Revised

THOMAS A CLARK
The Path to the Sea

TONY CURTIS
What Darkness Covers

JULIA DARLING
Sudden Collapses in Public Places
Apology for Absence

CHRISSIE GITTINS
Armature

MICHAEL HASLAM
The Music Laid Her Songs in Language
A Sinner Saved by Grace

JOEL LANE
Trouble in the Heartland

HERBERT LOMAS
The Vale of Todmorden

IAN POPLE
An Occasional Lean-to

SUBHADASSI
peeled

JACKIE WILLS
Fever Tree